Stalking Through Tall Grasses

by

Marie Scott

DORRANCE PUBLISHING CO
EST. 1920
PITTSBURGH, PENNSYLVANIA 15238

Dorrance Publishing Co
585 Alpha Drive
Suite 103
Pittsburgh, PA 15238
Visit our website at www.dorrancebookstore.com

ISBN: 979-8-88812-383-6
eISBN: 979-8-88812-883-1

An amazing, amazing, amazing book of poems. They touch my heart, they make me sing, they bring me to tears, and into laughter. Marie Scott hears the extraordinary in the ordinary as she writes of common things so thoughtfully, reflectively, colorfully–flowers in her garden, her sisters, her life, her father, the Minnesota woods, the fog, allowing everyday moments to transport us into poetic imaginings. Amba Z. Gale, Poet, Author, Teacher

I just got a copy of Dancing on the Wind. It's beautiful and two minutes in I was overcome with every emotion possible. That's what poetry is supposed to do, right? At least that's what this poetry does for me. Tim Hall, Engineer

Reading Marie Scott's poems is like speaking with a dear friend. The language of her poems is conversational, direct, simple. That's where the beauty of the poems in Dancing on the Wind lies, in their sparkling simplicity. Janice Bressler, Attorney

Thank you for your wonderful book of poetry. It is so delightful and funny and melancholy and observant and catching, both sad and hurtful and yet so joyous and even made me laugh out loud. Sharon May, Author's friend

Dedicated

to the wolf's howl

and

the lion's roar

〜〜〜

Stalking through tall grasses
on stealthy cat's feet
we seek the sparkling lure of life.
Intent, cautious,
alert to beauty, danger, prize,
we carefully pad our soft feet forward
through the jumble of loud voices calling out belief,
through the tangle of loves and hates,
to leap, to joyfully pounce, as
through the jungle of tall grasses
we stalk the clarion bell.

We hold this precious thing in our hand,
this thing called life,
so common we forget it's ours!
Let us celebrate it here
in this verse
in our hearts
in our collective awareness,
in this moment.
Let's allow the wondrous treasure of it
to alert us
to lift us into the vibrant joy
of our existence within its breath.
For we are alive, you and I,
alive!

Let me tell you something.
The sweet scent of orange blossoms.
The savory scent of mowed hay.
The wind in the trees.
Clouds scudding by.
If you stop,
to see, to hear, to smell,
something warm and wonderful
will stir your being here.

Silence has made itself heard this morning.
Silence more than the absence of the sound of his voice.
Silence that is the quiet in the motion of the air he once stirred,
the emptiness of the space he once inhabited.
It's the silence of being without him.
The silence of being alone.
A profound silence opening into
a citadel of stillness within my very self,
a new place wherein to stand,
to sit, to run, to play, to work, to think, to be still.
To be still in a quietness as strange, as potent, as life itself,
as potent, as spacious, as life with him.
Stillness tinged with sorrow.
Stillness shaded in jubilance
twin to our togetherness.

Peacefully sitting was I
beneath a canopy of leafy branches,
bright flowers painting out-of-doors with color.
A breeze lifted the branches and let them fall,
calling me from quiet reverie,
carrying me from stillness
to awareness of movement, change,
the rotation of the earth
shifting us, rearranging us, transforming us,
throughout our whole humanity.

Eye-level with the grass
there are no houses,
no buses, no people,
just the horizon,
a haze of fog
and sky and sea,
a twilight path
to dreams.

Another time,
rounding the crest of the hill,
the mouth of the bay
hazily painted in clouds and mist,
a brushstroke of quietness.

Brilliance of sunsets
or shining moon and stars
are not required
to lift our lives beyond strictures,
when the sweep
of mist-softened horizons
expand the heart.

Scatter to the wind grievances of the heart.
Let loose from the branch dry pods of shriveled hurts.
Enormous they seem, these fragile egos trembling on the vine,
these tangled trestles to which we cling, postulating happiness,
making us seem to be someone, something—
he will adore me, she will honor me, they will elevate me—
incantations sowing seeds of dissatisfaction.

Desist from composting anguish, tending grudges,
plucking them from the tender shoots of blossoming promises
into the potency of clear-eyed seeing, warm-hearted enterprises,
letting them fly from strong arms eager for loving embraces.

Within our hearts, within our homes, throughout our country,
within these troubled times,
good will must triumph.

He touched her cheek
to raise her gaze to his,
recognition full and sweet
before lowering his lips
in a tender, lingering kiss
not of arousal but of love,
a gaze, a kiss
to make love known,
true and deep,
precedent to passion.
Seems odd to need to be stated,
that caresses be communicated with love,
but so often between lovers
is a shyness to this opening of the heart.

⌒⌒

Short quick days,
dream-filled nights.

Sky blue. Sky cloudy.

A book in hand.

A trowel and watering can,
leafy trees aflutter,
birds tweeting, hopping cutely,
nibbling seeds fallen from blossoms,
wings awhirl while sipping nectar.

Dressed to kill
for a night on the town,
laughter and talk,
a glass of wine.

Sun rising in the east
descending in the west.

Short quick days,
dream-filled nights
lingering on color,
steadiness and flight.

⌘

Stalking through tall grasses.
Stalking, not tramping.
Crouching, waiting, watching.
Standing on tiptoe
to peer over grass tops,
seeking our bearings.
Stepping forward,
the rustle of grasses
brushing our legs.
Reaching across grasses
to clasp the hand of another.
Sleeping under the stars
in the moonlight,
the murmur of tall grasses,
whispering to our dreams.

The moon hovers outside my window,
low and bright,
hanging in the sky
as if it has nothing else to do,
as if it's everything unto itself.
And I feel myself hover,
low and bright,
casting a glow
as I hang here in the world
as if I had nothing else to do,
as if I am everything unto myself.

∽∾∽

Don't think traffic. Think people.
People like me. People like you.
Going places. Doing things.
All of us living on this earth,
traveling busy thoroughfares
together.

Fluttering in the breeze am I,
aimless.
I fix my feet upon the ground,
gaze upward
into the swaying branches of eucalyptus and cypress,
and join the rightful place of being here
fluttering in the breeze.

It's the breakers that catch the artist's eye,
finding the light in their swell,
the shape of the foam dancing to shore, beckoning,
stirring body and soul to romping gladness,
while the endless expanse of the great sea beyond,
gray or blue or silver, rippling or smooth as glass,
lightened or darkened depending on the day,
extending as background—there, drama hidden,
those waters of the deep pushing the breakers to shore.
As the eye roves beyond the foaming swells,
and rests upon the deep sweep into vastness,
there rises a mighty swell lapping at the shores of the heart,
plunging the soul into its depths.

⨳

"Hi, life," I said
to the stars above
to the green grass below
to the flow of the river
the splash of the sea
to the throb of my pulse
in the brush of breath
coloring the world with
life
life
spilling through time
animating my days
touching my heart
in gentle reassurance.
Oh, yes, on this quiet winter eve,
"hello," sweet life.

Do you think George Washington
ever in all his wildest dreams
imagined the people he enslaved
taking seats in government,
the natural consequence of him and his fellows
penning the Constitution of the United States?

Can you imagine the astonishment
felt by the People on this continent
in seeing white faces populating their earth?
And now today, do you see white faces blanch
as faces the color of those original inhabitants multiply,
taking residence in the homes of our land?

Can we imagine a United States
no longer of European descent by arrogant definition
but of the sweet mix of all the world?
And if we can imagine it,
how do we see this democracy progress,
change, expand, embrace, flourish anew—
as has been done from the time of George
to the time of now?

∻

Cradled in moss and ferns.
Young legs learning to walk,
stepping along pathways
pounded firm and sure
by older feet trod.
Stalking through tall grasses.
Branching pathways narrowing
into dark forests, widening into dry plains,
high mountain vistas opening to promise.
Rushing eagerly forward,
vines and roots tangling the tread,
making way through tall grasses.
Remarkable sojourn,
this long life ahead.

I wondered how a person could write a novel.
It seems so complex and marvelous.
I write words in phrases and snippets of thought.

Then I read that characters and plot-twists
come to the mind of the novelist
with a mind of their own.

I knew then that her words come
with the same unexpected urgency as mine,
whether story, or poem.

And I thought,
what wonderful worlds,
our minds.

When water pools and swirls around you
and you lose your footing—

when life turns upside down
and you hang like a bat from the ceiling, squeaking—

when the ground shakes beneath your feet
and everything around you goes squiggly—

when you get yourself righted again,
although somewhat askew—

when you marvel that things can get so mucked up
and you're still alive and kicking—

then you know it's going to be alright,
you've braved the worst and made it through.

I sing the song of you.
You flow through my blood,
sweat from my pores,
dance along my skin.
You wrap melody around my heart,
send me music from the light shining from your eyes.
I sing the song of you,
O my beloved.

Along the line of least resistance,
a trickle of spring water
carves a pathway
down the mountainside,
widening, deepening as it gathers momentum
tumbling over rocks, around boulders,
splashing from great heights,
winding through cool woodlands,
spanning vast plains, broad and lazy,
joining the great waters of the sea.

Hikers follow the pathway carved down the mountainside,
picnickers spread food and fellowship alongside tumbling streams,
waders in the cold rushing waters shout with pleasure,
travelers stand in awe at the glory of great falls,
stroll through woodlands along creek beds,
sail and row and swim in broad waters,
joyfully play at the seaside,
all unfettered
in the wanderings of least resistance.

ᔕᗢᔕ

It may sometimes seem you're simply waiting to die
retired from purposeful endeavors of youth.
But, oh, the splendor in that waiting—
wind and clouds and sea,
birds, butterflies, bees,
blossoms dancing in the breeze,
the animating touch of friends,
honeyed solitude singing, "you're alive,"
leisurely strolling at the edge of town,
 catching surprised glimpses of creatures of the wild—
right here, at the edges of the city,
the loping gait of the coyote,
the roly-poly lumbering of the raccoon.
Ah, yes, there are splendors in the waiting!

∽∽

I ate almonds with a blue jay today
in the cool foggy mists of morning.
He hops on a branch near where I'm sitting,
cocks his head and looks at me.
That's my cue to go into the house
for nuts he's shopping for.
I scatter them on the table between us,
he industriously planting them for another day,
memorizing where they lay.
We share moments and almonds,
this blue jay and me
in the cool foggy mists of a morning.

The lumbering giant raised his fists,
stomped across the small nation at his feet.
Others of the world raised their heads from squabbling,
opened their eyes to the threat—a moment of awakening.
"Freedom trembles at your fate, O small nation," they cried.
"We will put our differences aside to come to your aid,
match your courage with our own,
lift our sights beyond timid ventures,
make cooperation our rule of law."
Freedom from tyranny became the blue and yellow flag
flying unity for democracy drawing people together,
the giant's roaring devastation awakening humanity.

Long the journey begun for a free world order
where no longer rule kings, caesars, czars, dictators of any stripe
with power to slash the world into slave and master.
We have named the giants' footprints crimes against humanity, genocide.
International laws enacted by courageous people exist
providing the means for shooting the giant in the foot
bringing him down whenever he straddles the hemisphere
with his crime, destruction, and horror.
When we call for the world to be different,
we're not dreaming,
we're staking precedence.

Within democracy itself, change is alerted,
recognizing systems authorized to disenfranchise any but the elite.
Nowhere shall practices override just laws serving all the people.
Nations will strive for prosperity over greed, goodwill over power,
for white brothers and sisters to hear the cries
of their brown brothers and sisters,
for men and women to heed the voices of women
struggling under male rule,
a world for all those marginalized made equal,
bringing the day when even wars shall cease,
when nourishment replaces hunger,
when peace is preferred over anguish and harm,
when domination turns to dust.
When giants no longer roam the earth.

This is not a new song,
but an old one sung with renewed vigor.
Let us sing it lustily!

Parting tall grasses
to clear my way,
and still, tall grasses
as far as can be seen,
tangling, obscuring,
incessant sprouting.

Stalking through tall grasses,
taking steps forward,
sometimes finding a gem along the way,
or a room full of fun and laughter.
A decimated field of bodies
felled by death falling from the sky.
Tall buildings to enter.
Warm bodies to rest alongside.

The lifelong journey
through tall grasses
leading to the sea.

⌒⌒

The garden takes the brunt of my restlessness,
restlessness buzzing through my head,
razing my heart to a lazy discontent,
dancing in my limbs going nowhere.

I go to the garden, gaze with dissatisfaction
at what I once thrilled to plant in gorgeous disarray
Planning begins the turmoil of change.
Dig up that. Move this here. Open up space there.

In the absence of roads winding to adventure,
action shredded with meaning,
gatherings gathering me in,
arms, an embrace,
the garden as tapestry
is lure to restlessness.

The written word!
That inky realm wherein lies treasure.

By dint of press,
free thought and broad perception
expanded from only the learned elite
to the common learner, to everyone
—you and me—
the printing press leafleting the world.

And the library,
made free and scattered across the land,
wending its way through time and space
lending to any and all voices,
opening our closedness to humanity,
teaching the wonders of the world,
gloriously stretching our thinking and feeling—
these harbors of bookdom
handing us the printed word.

Inheritors of press and library,
thought, ideas, perception, stories
stirring our blood,
we look up to see the world around us
with eyes and hearts alive, alert;

we smile into our communities
with joy, with knowledge.

All because of the printing press
leafleting our lives,
and its sister, the library,
giving us a place of solitude
for opening its pages.

I rise of a morning
with a jangle of sound running through me.
Picking up my fiddle,
drawing the bow across the strings
of dread, drab and dreary,
drawing the bow across a ray of light,
a wisp of pleasure, a springing forth of joy,
until the music of myself
sings the song of my day
in a melody strung with color.

If there be a drop of pure thought
clear, poignant, timely
at the center of existence
then there be hope for humanity.

Be there a drop of pure thought
at the center of being
still and fully conscious,
then there be hope for me.

ᗢᗢᗢ

I wasn't really sure what love was.
I called it love
and kept him because he was here.

Announced it to the world:
"This man who is here
I love."

Never once let anyone
or myself doubt it,
the love for this man.

So assuredly declared,
how could it not be
that it was love.

While what I had all along
was this man,
maybe, maybe not love.

Until knowing him,
his being here,
became some sort of love.

Love that lasted
in its offhand way
throughout the years.

A treasured lovingness
that otherwise would not have been.
But it was, with his being here.

⤎⤏

The sound of water coming to shore.
Rays of sunlight through shaggy branches.
The scent of green growth dusted with the fragrance of wildflowers.
And the water — always the water—lake, river, creek, stream,
a wall of water falling from towering height.

Lying here now in moon and starlight,
the forests in shadow,
I'm softly wrapped in day's delight of
light and trees and water.

Oval-shaped, it was,

the space carved in the world

within which to rest,

from which to be whoever we were,

to do whatever we were doing.

And in that oval-shaped space

we were us, with a place in the world.

It really wasn't known to us

that the space was oval,

that it was carved for us, by us,

as our place in the world,

until he was gone

and I wander within its parameter

thus learning of its shape,

wander here because

it is the only shape I know,

so meticulously had we carved it.

I wander here in its emptiness

once filled to the brim with the life of us

but empty with just me in it.

I not empty,

but the space in which I dwell,

this oval-shaped circle of love,

this space that was the only space I knew.

Now, not filled,
I feel the rim of it
extending all around me
empty.

⌖

The best part of being lost is being found.
Found in a meadow dazzled with wildflowers.
Found on a mountaintop smothered in snow.
Found in the arms of a lover besotted with pleasure.
Found in the laughter of friendship.
Found in the pages of a good book.
Found on the street where you live.
Found wherever in this whole wide world
We may find ourselves lost.

Brown sugar sweetness,
rich dark molasses,
these soft memories
blending joy in buttery richness.

Memories crinkling the eyes
to seep tears of tenderness and loss,
fears' clutches, fury of angers, forgotten.
'Tis joy and sorrow visiting the heart
with their brown sugar sweetness,
their buttery richness.

Deep in thought,
worry creasing my brow,
thinking getting-on-in-life thoughts,
I glance out the window.
Mist touches treetops.
A soft stirring in my chest,
a softening of my face,
the worry-crease vanishing.
That mist in treetops
can deeply affect our being here
is a mystery
worthy of letting it settle
still and wondrous
in our breast.

Explorers hack through
        tangled forests,
                forge rushing rivers.
Like me, hacking through
        disappointments,
                forging chasms of uncertainty.
Them to discover
        something new,
                me to discover life.
They prepare
        with knowledge
                and anticipate discovery.
I prepare
        with wide-eyed fascination,
                and with verve.
Hack away,
        forge the unknown,
                I do,
urged on with
        the zest of the explorer
                within me.

The flutter of you across my heartstrings
reminds me to live life true
to the pleasure and goodness
crafted with you.

Stalking through tall grasses
to find the way to what?
to forage a pathway to where?
in this uncharted territory of living life.
Losing the way in grasses
tinging the hillsides ochre,
coloring the valleys maroon,
painting wide fields hazelnut brown,
swaying golden in rhythm with youth's heartbeat,
the dance of tall grasses beckoning in the breeze.
Arriving anew to the unknown.

With accomplishment wreathed in garlands wound through her hair,
the old woman smiles a secret smile of contentment
in her quiet life of moving her body for health and vigor,
tending her garden, its fragrance calling to birds, butterflies, and bees,
enjoying the company of sisters, nephews, nieces; of life-long friends,
wandering the pleasures of the city, the delights of the shoreline.
She watches the historic events of her country, her culture, the world,
balancing between despair at the dangers
and flourishing hope in the valiance toward
freedom, community, peace, humanity,
all the while hearing the whispers of her incoming life-ending time
from this world of anguish, wonder, and surprise.

✎

I don't know your tender places.
I thought because we were vowed to each other
that I knew you, such a part of you that I was.
I thought your tender places were mine to share.
But I trampled them without knowing the hurt I caused,
tender places being more tender, more veiled,
than I even knew of my own tender places also trampled.
O my beloved. Without knowing, we do each other harm.

Words evocative invoke an intake of breath,
shaping the world within our breast.
Coupling with thought or enlarged story well-told,
they encircle the mind and fling it to the stars,
stirring emotions in hands gentle as a lover's,
the human heart soaring as a bird in flight,
breathe shapes and colors into our own imagining,
catching the light of life surrendered to wonder,
dipping into depths dark and glistening.

"Hello, sea," I said,
having glanced out my window
as I perch on the hill above,
"Hello, you wide, wild ocean of the deep"
stretching to the horizon, breakers rolling to shore.
Wind whips the trees on the cliffs
dancing the song of the clouds overhead.
And I'm glad I glance up
to see this world so rich and alive
lending liveliness to me.

Intimacy. Let me sing your song!
Years and years within touch of another,
witness to each other day-in day-out.
Pleasure celebrated, discontent shared.
Talk nourished by understanding lived together.
Bodies joining, passions roused.
Making love with life, the laughter, the fun, the joy.
The fury, eye to eye, heated voices raised.
Annoying and endearing differences,
grievances accepted within arms' embrace.
Cozy, quiet moments, fingers tangled in hair,
when sad, when afraid,
muddling through worries, despair,
gaining courage from sturdy closeness,
love's glow radiating, steady, sure,
life and death held within my arms.

Rare, intimacy, I've discovered,
for so many never found,
absent altogether in the cacophony of world events,
hidden from the arena of social relationships, friendships,
though gems in their own right.

Let me sing the dirge of intimacy lost!
The stillness of the night, the bustle of day,
no measure against the ravishing hunger, the wolf's cry,
for intimacy.

Do you see me?
Or do you only see
the effects of aging
upon my body.
Do you see me?
Or do you only see
the color of my skin,
the texture of my hair.
Do you see me?
Or do you only see
my limp, my stutter,
my wheelchair.
Do you see me?
Or do you only see
my shyness, my aggressiveness,
my uncomfortableness here with you.
Do you see me?
Or do you only see
my popularity, my fashion sense,
my prettiness, handsomeness.
Do you see me?
Or do you only see
my homelessness, my poverty?
Or maybe my success, wealth, prestige?
Do you see me?
Or do you only see

snow and cold and vastness,
division, threat, hopelessness.
How shall we see?
Look! Look hard, look long.
Let us see what we're looking for.

〜〜

When I stopped seeking love
seemingly just out of reach,
I found in myself
its sweet song
singing there all along.
Then it was that
love came to me
bright and clear
from all around.

◊

Portend?—
this dream of you
come again and again
from many years past,
calling
through echoing chambers of time?
Portend of something significant, urgent,
something inspired,
something mysterious,
something profound?
Yes!
'twas the simple pleasure of seeing you again.

I float within whisperings I can't quite discern
while others speak clearly, stride boldly,
and change the world.
They stumble in cataclysmic proportion,
but press forward nevertheless
to discover and make real
that which carries us forward.

I float. I swim in warm waters,
drink from fresh springs,
dream dreamy dreams,
and wonder if between
the floating and the strokes of boldness
an invisible thread is weaving
the movement of the world.

If when unexpected pleasure usurps ponderous days,
a whoop of joy does not erupt from out my throat
to sing a dance along high hilltops.

If when the sweet man whose memory is failing
eagerly says, "Where shall we go this morning?"
and I say, "Turn left at the next light,"
and without any specified destination
we do not scour the countryside together,
laughing as we go.

If when I lay me down within the night
I cannot breach the shadowy void
to feel again the touch of my long-gone love.

When loneliness lays its longing upon my breast,
I do not mount a mighty steed
and race across wild meadows.

Then— then—
where would I be—
where would I be—

Up close, the light behind the eyes is seen,
feelings shape the face, shape the moment,
beauty otherwise unnoticed,
the solemnity of a life,
the liveliness of being together
informing appearances.

At a distance,
physical distance or the distance of comparisons,
from glancing impressions,
deducing deductions determining worth,
standards of appearance influence perception,
judgments are made,
intimacy lost, beauty unseen.

Up close
relationship lies.

ᔕᗩᔕ

Joy hovers in gray clouds
high above somber masked figures,
breath separated against persisting pandemic—
infection, illness, death.
            Along parkland pathways,
            people stroll in the fresh air,
            masked, keeping distance,
            smiling with their eyes.
Streets bedroll desperate people with nowhere for shelter,
their remaining possessions on their backs.
            The vaccinated take the pleasure of sharing a meal with friends.
Salesclerks stand idle in empty stores dreading loss of their livelihood.
Family's grieve loved ones lost to the virus.
            Children run laughing and playing in parks,
            parents relying on open spaces for safety.
Those employed, though secure in house and home,
helplessly feel the gloom rendering the city dreary and desolate.
            People walk the beaches with their dogs,
            for the moment, gladly, sea breezes
            blowing fears free of harm.
New wars threaten,
hatreds feed on despair, escalating troubles,
earth melts into warming oceans shuddering with disasters.
            The sun still shines luminous in the cool air,
            warming, refreshing families by the seashore.
A pall blurs normal moments, dampens spirits.
            High above, in gray clouds, joy hovers, waiting. Waiting.

Stalking Through Tall Grasses ~ 55

Lost,
the ring to the words.
The poet in me,
fled.
What of this drabness,
residue of flight.
Without the poet,
where the life.

❧

We were two people stumbling around in the dark,
you and me, you lovely, lovely man.
We didn't know we were wandering in the dark.
We thought we were living a new and exciting life
as we tootled along holding hands,
hanging onto each other
as if our lives depended on it,
really and truly depended on hanging on,
hanging on to each other.
We loved it, the hanging on
as we danced along
living our life.
We had our moments of strife,
hurts, bewilderments, misunderstandings,
disappointments, out and out affronts,
but our hanging on was the joy of living,
and as I look into my eyes, into my happy face,
here as I gaze into the mirror,
I'm overjoyed with the happiness of our hanging on,
our dancing along in the dark,
the light of day sparkling along our way.
Oh, I do, I do.
I do so love our hanging on,
holding hands as we danced along.

Boundless solitude of ancient forests
lost to a human-trampled world
lies nestled in hidden recesses of the heart,
in dreams of dark passages opening to sunlight,
in longing quietly tucked away
in timeless echoes
sounding human endeavor with thoughtful recompense
as to how to abound trampled boundless riches.

Weariness fogs the dot of joy
lodged at the center of the heart.
I languish, caught in lethargy.
Rousing myself within the foggy haze,
I make my way to joy's radiance,
where it shines warm and reassuring,
patiently waiting, perpetually vibrant,
in that dot at the center of the heart.

❧

Vengeful words.
Demeaning.
Hurtful.
Irrevocable.
Careless pebbles tossed thoughtlessly, angrily,
rippling in widening circles,
troubling the waters,
troubling our lives,
troubling our nation,
recklessly,
lastingly.
Too long we dismiss vengeful words,
dismiss their hurtfulness
poisoning our world.

With intimacy lost,
the coyote's mournful wail
vibrates within my breast.

Where can ever again be
the touch, the look,
the loving of living intimately?

The howl of the wolf
is my howl now,
howling my longing.

O rare and glorious days
of joining with another
lost to this wilderness of keening.

Relaxed and easy,
swinging gaily through life—
then, that tiny spot
in the center of my back
just behind my heart,
tight,
bruised.

Have I come to the time in my life
when the past calls to me more than the present
and with greater allure than the future,
providing solace to a somewhat weary heart,
reminiscences wrapped in completion
of substance if not consequence,
long fingers of consequence tickling the perplexing present,
complicating visions of the future.

For the historical novel has become my favorite read,
where characters from real life elucidate what is known,
giving pause to the uncertainties in our changing world.
Where once stories danced with speculation
caught my imagination in a thrilling swirl,
spun thought into provocative questions,
created realms of possibilities,
I now lazily surrender to stories which resurrect
lives once lived to entertain me from ages past.

Has the future become so bleak, so fraught with terrors?
Or have I come to a particular time in my life
when enchanting stories for what might be,
where pitfalls and foolishness, hurtfulness and violence,
glamor, gaiety, adventure, heroic striving,
once incited visions of progress, newness, foretelling,
seem repetitive and dull, seem larger than their promise?

Have I reached that time
when my father could not feel the excitement I was living
in the age of my youth?

History tells me the future of today
will be the history of tomorrow, just as always.
That doomsday, end of the world, has always been the forecast.
That my melancholy is the time of my life come round.
Okay, then, let me luxuriate in historical novels,
discern the threads of yesteryear woven into the fabric of today,
discern which threads to cut loose
and which to weave in,
while at the same time opening myself
to new stories singing their songs into humankind.
Ah! Now I see. I've come to the time in my life of DISCERNMENT,
needing stories of the past to inform my present,
needing stories of the past and the present
to step into an abundant future.

A poet lived in the Heights of San Francisco.
She lived in a house modest for the Heights
but an elegant home nonetheless
with shutters the color of the sun.

Across the way in a mansion of a house
lofty with wealth and stature, rare open lands adjoining,
lived a handsome young man, the poet's playmate since a lad.
He and his horse raced with an abandon that bespoke his character,
abandon which thrilled the heart of the gentle poet,
his wild hair flying in his love of galloping recklessly.
From childhood through budding womanhood,
they rode together, he holding her tight before him,
racing through forest pathways along cliffs above the sea.

Always she knew he loved her true,
inspiring the words that made her a poet.
One day, the boy-become-man riding alone, the horse stumbled,
sending him flying over the cliffs to the rocky beach below.
The empty mansion crumbling in grief in view from her latticed window,
the gentle poet in the modest sun-shuttered house
penned poems singing the songs of love lost,
the phantom of a wild-haired boy in eager excitement
racing through forests, along cliffs high above the sea.

Self-Doubt

From within,
prowess
surge of confidence
flash of brilliance.
From without,
a glance of approval
a word of praise.

Shadow hovers,
elusive, unbidden,
dimming the brightness,
shrinking the promise,
summoned from somewhere
inexorable
pervasive
persuasive

Victor.

A curling inward,
retreat
defeat.

In every rock and flower, the whisper of him.
In every passing shape and form, the dream of him.
Reaching into time, reaching into memory,
with long fingers sculpting our weight and tenure
to bring him more and more home
in this vast empire of castles and foam.
Where have you wandered to?
When are you hastening back?
O my eternal beloved, ever returning to me.

When light slants through the sky just so
or clouds hover awaiting their flare of glory in the setting sun,
there stirs a likeness in the tenders of the heart
spinning tendrils of substance ethereal
within this world wherein we dwell,
sustenance within the veil of flesh.
For though we cast ourselves uniquely superior,
our heartstrings bind to greater things—
a play of light, the turning of a leaf, churning surf.

A TENDER MOMENT
WITNESSED BY A PASSERBY

Narrow ledges and rocky climbs,

the so-small little girl clamoring up,

tight rope walking the itsy spaces,

wending her way down,

animated, alive in the thrill of it.

Mountain height for her.

Within arms-reach for her father pacing alongside,

but stepped back far enough

to give freedom for her own navigation,

for finding her own balance,

exercising her skill, will,

learning risk, learning trust,

delighting in the strength of her own volition.

I love loving-kindness.
It's my favorite thing in all the world.
It's the color of rainbows,
fluffy as clouds, solid as earth,
our eyes its revelation,
our behavior its embrace.
Tough and tender, radiating warmth
through layers of protection against the cold,
we can safely settle into it completely.
The best thing in the world, loving-kindness.

I lightly touch you with my fingertips,
your silky skin and steady heartbeat.

I touch you with my fingertips,
your passion, hopes, and dreams,
your loneliness, your love.

I touch you with my fingertips,
fall into you, the fullness of you,
the shining brilliance of happiness.

I touch you with my fingertips,
release you to the arms of death,
shatter into tiny glistening shards.

⌒⌒⌒

The storm broods.
A shout dances through us.
Horses flare their nostrils,
manes and tails whip in the wind,
they lift their heads, they run—run.
We lift our eyes to the excitement.
The headlands a purple hue in the misty haze,
dark clouds amass shapes voluminous, thunderous, majestic.
Incongruent promise, the quiet rainbow smiling from the roiling sea-
green sea.
Our blood stirs.
Dance, prance
in joyous exhilaration.
Run—run,
run free,
muscles flexing,
the wind in our hair.

༚༚༚

A madman who quite simply is simply not stopped.
We saw it before, we're seeing it again—
a short man with a short mustache then,
a large man with a bad hairdo now,
rising, rising, rising in power, setbacks notwithstanding,
an uncanny rise, atrocities overlooked,
shadowy forces propelling disaster.

We're celebrating a reprieve, counterpoint is at play,
but danger largely hidden simultaneously amplifies.
One half of our two political parties are not seeing
the harbinger of horror, continue to embrace
the simmering toxic autocratic stew,
not recognizing what seems inescapably obvious.

Not calling it, not stopping it, amplifying the danger.

We've lived this before, vowed never to live it again,
and here we are.

At times of distress, the expert said,
nature offers solace. We turn to it instinctively.
The magentas, oranges, pinks, and golds of sunsets
are not just beautiful, they shimmer on our skin.
The curl of the ocean rushing toward us
isn't just ebb and flow, but washes through us.
Birds in flight are the soaring of our own spirit.
The vibrant green of grasses after spring rains,
the towering of great forests,
the scent of flowers, breezes lifting our hair,
the fluttering leaves of the trees, everything everywhere
entering the fissures of our fractured hearts.

The sky was blue
with a shining sun,
the ocean stretched clear and calm.

A breeze began to stir.

Way out beyond the calm sea,
piles of gray clouds massed
into a thick white bank
sitting atop the thin lips of the horizon.

A waiting,
waiting on change in the atmosphere.

～

Trudging, I was, bones creaking.
Rather than carry me along the hillside,
limbs longed to lay themselves down.

I felt the breeze brush my cheek.
I saw the spring green of the grasses.
Budding of blossoms enchanted.
Then came an exchange of friendly greeting
with a young woman gaily striding toward me;
and a word and smile with a dog-walker passing by,
his clutch of leashes attached to frisky, smiling dogs.

My bones became less creaky, my limbs more limber,
my heart sang a renewed song.
"So glad I'm taking a walk today,"
it happily sang to me.

There's something about being alone that satisfies.
Stillness. Room to expand.
Thought wandering without interruption.
Skin relaxing, no longer on point.
There's also something initially disconcerting
about being alone always and forever,
but then the inevitable settles in,
this new way of being blossoms.

You get to know yourself. Get to know yourself
in the way of acquainting yourself with an attractive stranger,
without worried glances at yourself, without sidelong looks
in relation to everyone around you, measuring up,
fitting in, being who you think you should be.

Others are not excluded in life alone,
welcoming visits to chat, to travel,
to enjoy a meal together, embark on an adventure.
But then to return to solitude wrapping 'round,
to move once again at your own satisfying pace.

Not that living with a beloved isn't wonderful.
It is. The sharing of real closeness.
Thoroughly knowing another, being known.
Someone alongside you standing witness to life.
Someone who loves you.

Alone, together intimately, socially,
all testament to an elasticity, a richness,
an adaptability, an expansive capability,
a varied gracious beauty to us lifelong beings.

No quietness in the silence of pandemic cautions
stilling the noisy restlessness of dampened desires,
constraining movement, a world distanced.
Weeks to months to years
and still masked, we walk the streets
careful not to breathe the breath of closeness.
Liveliness submerged in restriction,
the machine of survival grinding on,
we dip deep into perseverance,
into courage mustered in footsteps
silently echoing solitary walks.

Through the layer of clouds
the sun finds a break,
spotlighting the houses on the hill.
As the sun dips toward the sea
a puff of cloud brightens,
drifting across the layered gray.
Such a regular thing, in a day, these shifts,
and yet to witness, to watch, to see
doesn't seem regular at all.

~∽~

If a robot is smarter than me.
If it can do things faster and better than me.
Which it is. Which it can.
What about me?

Robots can line up kindergarteners,
link them together for safety,
walk them off on a field trip
pointing out this or that designed for them to learn.

Then I saw the children loosed from tethers,
saw their teacher laugh, make eye contact,
heard her nuanced words reach their sensibilities,
recognized human touches not replicable.

I look into your eyes,
I see your smile,
I hear the timbre of your voice,
I feel your arms around me.

The robot's voice simulates a human voice
but it is not your voice.
Then is when I know who I am.
Who we all are. Who we always shall be.

✎

There's the love of your life, of course,
that amazing dance with its foibles, its intimacy.
There's the love of parents, siblings, children.
There's the love that flourishes in nooks and crannies unexpectedly,
the delight on a child's face, the generosity of another,
literature stirring the depths of us,
birdsong, flowering meadows, fluttering treetops, clouds.
When love fills the breast in its myriad ways,
surprising us in its persistence through thrum and discord,
the flush of feeling it inspires
lifts to where humans are supposed to go,
rounds us out and settles us in,
happy deep, deep down.

◦◦◦

You read a story,
an easy-reading book
that moves along, entertaining,
a story about these people
in these situations
in this time and place,
people not unlike you
but not exactly like you, either.
You get involved in their lives,
their hopes and dreams,
disappointments, disasters,
thoughts and feelings
not unlike yours
but not exactly the same.
You read another story,
another and another,
and then it's happened,
you've opened somewhere
you weren't open before.
Book are subversive,
but oh, in such a good way!

I'm a freethinker.
I adhere to no belief system,
practice no discipline.
Not peering through any scrim of thought,
rents in what scrim there be opening to new vistas,
I swing free.
This freedom, this joy,
connects me to everything around me,
has me singing lustily, happily,
has me dancing through midnight blue
and sparkling silver.

⤬

Exhilarating seaside morning!
The curling of the sea to shore.
Hair ruffling in the breeze.
Sea birds dipping low, floating high.

"The ignorance of dominance,"
the phrase lingers on my lips,
the very nature of dominance
making it impossible for the dominant
to have the slightest inkling of knowledge or understanding
about the real selves of those they dominate.
When I lived in Idaho, people used the word "ignorant"
when they meant rude or insulting.
The ignorance of dominance is certainly that,
but I'm thinking of it here in its dictionary definition,
"lacking knowledge, education, or experience."
The trouble—well, one of the many troubles—with
the ignorance of dominance
is the ignorance of the dominant that they are ignorant,
ignorant without their even knowing they are insulting,
rudeness under cover of self-appointed rightness,
rightness based on ignorance they don't even know is theirs.
It perpetuates such harm,
this ignorant rude insult.

Here we lay
with sweet-smelling grasses
swaying in the breeze,
the smell of the sun on your skin.
O these golden days
when our hearts are gay
and our love lies tender.

Wending our way through the days,
shapes and patterns of life shared in
tittle tattle, careful observations,
work, play, romping in glades,
strolling along stream beds,
flinging arms wide
to embrace the flow of the sea.
When these murmurs soft and sweet,
heard, spoken, ceased,
words sang the music
where our love and laughter once sang,
poems heralded the living of life
to hold in my hands shapes and patterns,
tender nuance, breadth, depth.

Once on a spring evening when
things in bloom scented the air with freshness,
the glow of the sunset turned things rosy,
breezes touched the skin in carefree caress,
changing of seasons came to mind,
contemplatively lengthened into ages past,
rounded back into the present,
stretching toward the future.

Time and seasons irrepressible.
Wonderment at the dot of me
sitting in a spring evening
within a moment of time turning,
lifting me up, carrying me away,
setting me down again
into breezes, blossoms, and sunset.

❦

An old-time melody heard by lonely and broken men
stirred memories of youth and promise and laughter—
the softness, loveliness, gaiety of then,
tenderness for heartstrings taut with weariness now.
To the words of the melody they raised their shaky voices
resonant with forgiveness of harsh cruelties endured,
the moment of melody lifting the heart from strain.

In the quiet of early morning
I breathe in the stillness,
step closer to the tree.
It is standing near the pine bough
that I see newly blooming pinecones
unnoticed, standing at a distance.
Attracted to the heady, spicy scent
of Mexican marigolds at my shoulder
I swoon in the dew-laden pleasure
of this quiet early morning.

I look out across our country with sorrow.
How could our America the Beautiful
find itself in such deadlock
between democracy and the threat of tyranny?
Then I count the many ways
of the blurring of our treachery
and see that it comes now to face us.
For freedom to ring true,
this is the day of reckoning.

With a brush of pine needles against the sky,
lifted briefly by the wind,
a shift occurred. Striving quieted,
the commonplace suddenly transported
to where dwells a sense of satisfaction.
It is named joy, this breezy flutter within,
lifting me
as pine needles lift
to brush against the sky.

Out in the firmament
with the dusky rose
and the fresh-smelling sea,
out where
the ocean touches the sky
with birds flying by
and stars in swirly array,
the music of creation
sings into the spheres
and we dance in the moonlight,
we float and we fly
as we catch hold
and hang on
to the buzzing and swooning
of being alive.

‏‏⸙

Imagine it.

What if it became popular for us to understand the other guy?

That's not what we do.

What we do is try to get the other guy to understand us.

But what if it gave us satisfaction—became popular—

for us to understand the other guy

while conversely, the other guy found satisfaction

in understanding us.

It could happen, 1st, I think, if we wanted it to,

and 2nd, if we made it a practice to listen.

Of course, this wouldn't be the only way to talk with each other,

but on the important stuff, here's how it might go.

You would say what was true for you—true deep down.

I would listen—just listen—

listen without rehearsing what I was going to say in return.

Then I would check to see if I understood you.

I would say, "you..." whatever I had heard.

You would confirm that what I heard was what you meant,

or that what I heard was not what you meant.

You would say, "That's right."

Or you would say, "That's not quite what I meant,"

and you would say again what you meant—what was true for you.

In saying it, it would come clearer to you and to me.

This would continue until I truly heard what was true for you—

heard with my ears, my mind, my heart, all my sensibilities,

because 3rd, I would have been present to listen—
I wouldn't be thinking about what I felt, thought, would say next,
I'd just listen. I would hear.
Once I had truly heard you, I would say what is true for me.
You would say, "You..." whatever you had heard.
I would say yes or no as the case would be.
This would continue, each of us hearing and speaking
for the purpose of understanding what was true for each of us.

When I understand what is true for you
and you understand what is true for you—
when you understand what is true for me
and I understand what is true for me—
and we speak this with each other—
we are in a space of understanding—
understanding more clearly than ever before.
Understanding is now what is between us.
Understanding is the power in which we are standing.
The power of understanding
is now what guides our next step with each other—
guides our being together.
Imagine it!

I must confess.
A select few others and I have done this.
When we did this, something new emerged

that carried us to a new place within ourselves,
in relationship with each other.
Things moved forward between us refreshed, renewed, transcended.
It may seem tedious. And it does take intention and concentration.
But it is also exhilarating.

Let's try it! Let's get good at it!
It changes us for the better.

Opening the door,
stepping into a spring morning,
the sun warming soft breezes,
bees buzzing among opening blossoms
is to step into freshness, lightness,
into a gladdening of the heart.

Let long be the slumber
and sweet the dream
of this life on this earth
with its mountaintops,
its oceans stretching to the horizons,
with rough and tumble humans
roaming and settling, warring and loving,
animals foraging, insects pollinating,
plant life in abundance.
Let long and sweet be this romp
slung across the skies,
rotating through the seasons,
time tossing us to the wind.
For where else such grandeur,
such breadth and depth of wonder be ours,
where else such solace for murmurings of the heart.

Cast in arbitrary nets
wherein we encounter each other with hatred, harm, and privilege,
we're learning—oh, we're learning
through these ages of too, too slowly
recognizing your dusky face alongside my pale one,
recognizing your muscular body alongside my soft one,
recognizing your fine mind alongside my equally fine one,
recognizing ourselves heart to heart.

Cast in nets of suffering, horror, mortal battle,
we rise from the ashes on sparks of humanity
bursting into blazing fires of our utmost promise,
promise of life together everlasting—you and I—
dark and fair, firm and soft, vigorous and needing an arm to lean upon,
your warm brown eyes meeting my blue ones with dancing tenderness,
your soft curvaceousness breathing comradeship to my strong hands,
your traditions and folkways singing songs alongside mine,
our lives renewed with combat abated,
fear skittered to the netherlands
by trust, belief in one another, love,
your very self inhabiting my world and mine yours,
making it our world.

This life!
Mingling wonder, sorrow, angst, joy.
Stalking through tall grasses obscuring vistas,
lost in labyrinths of wandering pathways,
standing on mountaintops seeing clearly.
This life of boredom,
of surprises, love, and loss,
sudden revelations.
This irreplaceable life!

Beneath the trees
the world brightens,
glimpses of ocean,
breath expands.

The world sings its songs
in rhythms and rhymes that are poetry.
The flutter of leaves, oceans surge and flow,
snow falls, whitening the landscape,
green shoots rise from warming soil
sending gay color of leaf and blossom swaying in soft breezes
as we stroll dense forests,
climb to mountaintops,
listen to birdsong.

‚‚‚‚

The young woman
opening to the world
rosy with promise
a beloved on the horizon
all of life glorious before her.

The maturing woman
accomplished in matters that matter
wending her way through
surprises appalling, enriching, adoring,
filling life to its fullest.

The old woman
rich in memories
life lived and living still
tenderly holding in her hands
the golden orb of fleeting days.

When the sky flames brilliance in the setting sun,
when leaves shivered by the wind still with dusk's calming
and I think of you,
then my heart warms golden
curls 'round itself in dusky restfulness
content in loveliness.

∽∾∽

You get awards and prestige titles
as a "contemporary writer"
if your writing is terse and gloomy,
if you speak of inadequacy and cruelty,
if you're a bit crass, a bit loony, graphic, and gross,
sketching weakness in the severe lines of the starkness of humanity.
Most likely it's important to render our foibles forlorn, brutal,
to give definition to our disappointing, disappointed selves,
to make our lacking visible and sharp in our awareness.

There is another contemporary writer
who also receives awards and prestige
whose writing is gentle, kind,
observant of things other than ugly or crude,
whose writing isn't romantic or sentimental,
which I'm supposing "contemporary writers" are avoiding,
but who writes of life as most of us live it,
an author's subtle sensibilities and keen eye
enlarging rather than diminishing us, lending a lift to existence.
This writer is my favorite,
for what do we have if not this.

A writer told a writing class that
writers have only one story,
a story written in an assortment of tones and nuances
with varieties of characters,
but still just one story.
She was speaking to writers,
but my thoughts turned to all of us,
each with our one story
to be told well in all its twists and turns
through all the years of our life.

Poems that shout history,
that shine a light on injustice,
that tell of hurts and harms,
that promise change,
promote progress,
are poems which inspire,
stirring the human heart,
enlightening the human mind.
These poems of import and meaning
are poems to be heralded far and wide.

My poems are quiet poems,
of little import,
perhaps lending a touch of tenderness,
perhaps connecting with the human spirit,
poems easy to overlook.
I wish to write poems
that expand the imagination,
reach for worlds beyond the suffering of this one.
poems that stretch us,
move us beyond ourselves.

Truth be told,
don't know what my poems do,
but every once in awhile
they seem to startle in their simplicity,
their wondering and wandering,
their stalking through tall grasses
with no clear sight in view.
Don't know why they should speak at all,
but they keep insisting that they should.

Bushy-browed clouds massing on the brow of the headlands.
Blue sky, their crown, puffy white clouds for ribbons in its hair.
At the feet, vast ocean waters, green breakers rolling to shore
from where suddenly, seagulls rise in a flock and swoop.
A mood in the air, a feel of the world layered in atmosphere
of grays, charcoal, azure, lavender blues,
layerings of the aliveness within us.

◦◦◦

Early morning light.
Dusk flirting with the night.
Transitions, entryways, closings,
enormity of existence
calling to the human heart,
softly wrapping delight
in the purity of shifting light.

Where will we stand in history?
Will we be in the white mob,
fists clenched, face contorted in hateful snarl,
screaming hurtful epitaphs at the tiny figure of a little black girl
who walks for protection between National Guard officers,
big men, uniformed, armed, alongside this tiny brave little girl?
Will we be screaming at a little girl because she's entering a public
schoolhouse,
an American schoolhouse erected for the education of all Americans,
a schoolhouse which the white mob deems theirs alone?
Look closely at the photos recording that historic event. Are we there?

Today, do we think Black Lives Matter,
or do we support scrubbing out of history,
out of consciousness, out of conscience,
the lives, the stories, of those who arrived in our country in chains,
of those whose land we stole and way of life we plundered?
Do we support hiding the laws, policies, practices
which have disenfranchised generations of American citizens,
believing our heritage to only be
the victories, perspectives, powers of white people?
Are we raising placards, raising our voices
to prevent the teaching of "critical race theory" in our schools,
falsely claiming that by including all our history in school curriculum,
white children are taught that they are racist?—
such a fervent objection strangely telling.

Or do we see the web of oppression woven into our country
needing to be teased out so that the fabric of our experience
can be woven into new patterns of wrongs righted,
becoming silver threads shimmering
with hope and justice and community?
Are we standing on the side of history striving to keep some folks down,
or are we standing for learning hard lessons to assure freedom for all?

On a sudden freshness to the air
life itself breathes its sweet breath,
be we ameba or upright creature,
radiating life's glow beyond all reckoning,
enlivening nature, humanity, city streets.

Having squandered this blessed heritage,
doomed ourselves toward extinction,
should we dare to surmise that earth,
having replenished itself from previous wastes,
will reconcile our tragedy with life anew?
Oh, anguished hopefulness.

In this propitious moment now,
oh exultant happiness,
you and I can relish the thought that we are part
of this sweet breath of life
carried to us on a freshness in the air.

There lingers in the air
this springtime evening
the spicy scent of marigolds
and the golden rays
of the setting sun
as you and I
in each other's arms
sway to the strains of soft music.

On a cold winter day
in the thin light
of watery dawn
the warm memory lingers
of a springtime evening
golden with loveliness.

Now here's a turn of event worth noting!
"Victoria's Secret," a mega-image,
mega-empire of women's lingerie,
has made public statement that it
created itself for men's sexual fantasies
and that its success has stumbled,
requiring it to assess anew
where lies the market for women's lingerie,
finding that it lies with women,
women who respect themselves,
who define themselves beyond men's fantasies,
earning money on their own behalf
spending it on lingerie as they prefer it.
Having discovered the Secret of woman-power,
Victoria's secret is to reimagine itself.
Setting aside the disturbing fact
that it made a fortune on its original intent,
how refreshing it is to see an industry,
long objectifying women,
turn to women for women's sake.

Turquoise it was,
startling in its surprising color
arresting the senses
as it lay at the feet of
familiar subtle grays tinged in
faint blush from the setting sun
darkening into night
this eve,
this one remarkable turquoise leaving of a day
among all the remarkable variances
of the sea and the sky and the turning of time,
the atmospheric pageantry
of cloud formations; plays of light,
bursting into glories of beauty
nurturing us with delight.

∽∾∾

You—heart of my heart,
whose footsteps matched mine,
side by side, arm in arm, cheek to cheek,
warm caress in the night.
Gone you are now,
yet your song lingers on,
phantom breath brushing my skin, fingers in my hair,
your sturdy self, your amused grace, your love, your loveliness,
O heart of my forlorn heart.

They were in their garage tinkering
as men are wont to do,
but these boys were playing with something new.
These boys were inventing a Technological Revolution.

I had to wake up in time to catch the plane.
"Hey, Siri," I said to the inert object in my hand,
"Set my alarm for 6am."
"Your alarm is set for 6am," a voice said.
At 6am my alarm rang
and I pressed "Stop Alarm"
and it stopped.

In an instant
a Siri I've never met, nor can I ever,
set my alarm and awakened me
all because these boys
were tinkering in their garage.

Stalking through tall grasses,
having lost my way,
I curl beneath a starry sky
to the chirping of crickets
and the conversations of frogs.
In morning's light
I bundle thoughts and belongings,
wend my way within wet bogs and dry grasslands
until I cross a pathway leading to my heart
sheltered by sunsets and whisperings of dawn.

When the moon
was a maiden, a lady, a crone
before the footfall claimed her
as a small step for man—
when the moon
shone promises from ages past
lighting the way for woman present
to shine whole and free in a new age,
shone for she who roamed this earth
from the beginning of time
alongside he who took its riches
while he stayed her hand, her heart, her mind—
when the moon
maiden, lady, crone
shone her light into the darkness
and woman woke from long slumber
to claim her power, to claim herself—
this was the day I was born to,
lay witness to a moment of time
when standing in moonlight by the sea
the wind in our hair
we sang songs as ancient as blown sands,
leapt free of bondage grown too heavy to bear,
danced in the light of the
maiden, the lady, the crone.

⌘

Small birds large in number
swirl, dip, swoop dark across the pale sky,
choreography of synchronized motion.

We've all seen it and marveled.

Then something caught my eye.

Clusters of us at the seashore,
colorful tracings across sandy sands,
a frolicking gambol in concert.

～∾～

Each blossom lasts but for a day.
Each day a new blossom blooms.
The hibiscus of abundant beauty
ever fading, ever blossoming.

Each person lasts but a day,
and every day a new person blossoms,
a world of abundant beauty
ever fading, ever blossoming.

Dreary thoughts drag at bright spiritedness,
the world throwing tantrums like a two-year-old,
terrorists, tyrants, typhoons, tornadoes,
fires ablaze, snow-caps melting, oceans rising.

Through the smoky haze you wend your way to me,
cheerful, bouncing with goodness, with laughter,
your love dispelling disasters sway,
your heart ringing true, if not righting the world, refreshing it anew.
As persistent through time immemorial as the horrors that abound,
always, always, the sun breaking through.

Gossamer fairy wings
brush against my skin
with their airy touch.
Invisible touches taking me unaware
gladdening my heart
lending life its tenderness.
From whence do they come unbidden
beyond precept and belief?
That is the mystery
ethereal and magical,
reminder from the nether worlds,
of the pleasure of pure delight.

∽∼∽

When I imagine me in this life,
I find my place,
can see my substance,
my shape of being.
It is disconcerting to be left alone
with no conventions
such as parenthood,
such as office,
such as marriage,
another person side by side,
no one to tether to,
a life with definition,
with context and image,
with prescription—
as in pre-scripted.
But this aloneness,
this wandering aimlessness
coming after a life fully lived,
needs imagination,
and imagined, it becomes
a life worth living anew
on new terms
coined by oneself.
Could be a life
flamboyant, engaged.

Could be a life
quiet, withdrawn.
Could be neither of these,
but a life lived with a subtlety
carved by the heart,
cunning, intensely felt,
harmonious.

In this moment, here,
I step outside into soft wisps of mists in the trees,
step into a speaking of more than words spoken,
all motion within me ceasing, a stillness awakening me,
poetry singing songs into realms of my heart
where dwells my lesser expressed livingness.
I reflect upon the balance we must keep within the swirls of conversation,
our attention taken in listening and responding,
initiating interaction and understanding responses,
the broad strokes of living overtaking the quiet moorings
hidden beneath bolder shapes and colors, accustomed sounds and rhythms.
When poetry from wherever speaks to the more within us,
resonates in startled awareness with what we overlook
and meets a newness in the pores of our being,
then, oh sing on, you poetry of the mists,
that we may reach whispered existence
stretching our lives in new dimensions.

I kept reaching for a tissue,
tearing at the corners of my eyes.
I weep seeping tears
squeezed from a heart tight with an anguish
hidden so deeply within my breast
there is no way to cry outright.
These are furtive tears of a national dimension,
of historic proportion,
brought by events of injustice made clear,
by human despair from one group abusing another group,
suffering disclosed in terms undeniable
which finally, finally is so tenderly wrought
as to awaken an entire nation
to see with new eyes, with new hearts.

Staring straight ahead
or busy on phones,
certainly no one smiling,
no eyes warming into feeling,
all of us neighbors far and near
unknown to each other
riding together on this city bus.

Suddenly, in my imagination,
a song springs forth
with a jaunty tune,
words easy to remember,
a song singing togetherness,
singing of joy in being alive,
singing of one another,
our burdens and cares,
our hopes and dreams,
our recognition of each other.
Rousing,
rousing us from stupor
from separateness,
from strangers,

we neighbors
all across the city
rejoicing our moment together,
singing songs as we ride along.

An unlikely idea,
a wonderful thought,
for if we begin singing,
we people of America,
would our songs ease
our loneliness, our estrangement,
our aggravations, our strife?
Would we become a happier,
healthier, nation,
if we were singing?

It may be that
if in our troubled hours
we don't have songs to sing,
we could lose our singing voices,
we could lose our way.

As proud City on the hill
vibrates the hum of
cumulated motion, sound—
stop. You can feel it—
so does my heartbeat,
brave face,
Camelot of Being Here,
vibrate cumulated living,
wanderings, wonderings,
tucked away sorrows, hopefulness, tenderness,
rendering their hum a distant thrum—
stop. You can feel it.

You come to me with such ardor,
the fresh smell of forest and sea in your hair.
You come to me troubled,
the musky scent of anguish on your skin.
You come to me tenderly,
reaching for me earnestly.
You come to me,
laughter and love in your eyes.
You come to me.
O my beloved.

If in the flow of blood through my veins
I cannot feel the murmur of the river,
the whisper of the wind,
the thunder of the tides.
If I cannot feel within the beating of my heart
the brightness of sunlight,
the glowering of darkening clouds,
the wolf's howl.
If my skin does not reflect
the shimmer of blossoms,
the warmth of summer breezes,
the shiver of winter cold,
Then surely I live in vain.

Astonished we are
at the number of stars in the sky,
tiny flames of light.
Were each of us,
each plant, animal, human,
a flame of light,
and certainly we are
when you think of the
bright life we each contain,
the starry night looking down
astonished must be.

"In the spirit of the thing," they say,
and they mean that subtle spritely thing
that inflames the moment with splendor.
When sparked with the spirit of the thing,
something quite mundane, you see,
suddenly radiates, glows,
and you come alive,
it comes alive,
whoever, whatever, is there in that moment,
comes alive for you.
That's when learning is understanding,
when the street is peopled by movement splayed in rainbows,
when weather is horses running with their tails held high.
That's when kissing is more than lips touching,
when touching is more than fingers on your skin,
when smiling is more than the showing of teeth,
when loving is truly loving.
O, the spirit of the thing.
Nothing can compare.

Love me with your eyes.
I don't mean look me over.
I don't mean assess my beauty
in terms of the value of my looks.
Love me with your eyes
reflecting your heart,
beholding me as who you love.
For without loving me with your eyes,
truly beholding me wrapped around your heart,
you are not loving me at all.

Stalking through tall grasses,
a predator not of killing, domination,
devouring other living things,
but for pouncing on meaning for sustenance,
ferreting out enlarged thought, perspective,
stealthily seeking tender reaches of the heart
then curling into loving embrace,
leaping, wrestling, romping, playing,
stalking sweet delights.

Not only does a tangle of shouting young boys
run pell mell after the fire truck with its clangorous wail,
barks and howls resound in noisy chorus,
echoing throughout the neighborhood
as household hounds join the fray.
Although the siren moan bespeaks alarm,
a quirk of a smile cannot be suppressed
at such raucousness so innocent of grief.

In the chambers of the heart
wherein doth lie the secrets of the soul
I one day found a loneliness covered over
with scraggly nuances of confidence nurtured by necessity.
Bluster and bravado had lurched forward a life
seen as noble and worthy of respect
draped in finery of grand words and excellent deeds
while hidden shivering and sad
a lonely quietness shorn of artifice graceless and still
encased a vibrant jewel of sincerity quite radiant
beneath drab reticence of abandoned self.
I knelt beside this lonely specter and gazed into its depth
enraptured by the contrast of glory and quietude.
I extended a gentle hand of affection and curiosity
and felt its surge of wisdom and isolation,
felt existence larger than appearances,
smaller than efforts of survival,
warmer than the beating of the heart within my own breast.
A wrenching cry of anguish rose within me at the loss I bore
in betrayal of the slender shadow of myself.

O the seemingly inevitable destruction.
Who thought Rome would burn.
Who thought Northern California would burn.
Who thought wind and water and fire
would be so fierce, so persistent that no government
however democratic or tyrannical could save its citizens.
Who thought that strife among people would circle the earth
with such devastation and heartache
as to decimate whole populations.
Who could imagine a hole in the heavens that would melt ice
and leave round white polar bears emaciated.
Who thought that first taste of pleasure,
of sweet perfumes and gentle breezes,
of forests and rivers and copses of green havens,
could shift into the path of such destruction.
O sorrow.

Nine years past,
your leaving this world.
Still, my body remembering,
I feel you wrapped 'round me.
Still, my heart swoons at the thought of you.
I hear your laughter along with mine
at the ironies of life.
Sitting beneath the moon,
I feel your soft breath.
Striding boldly in the sunshine,
I lean upon your strong arm.
Nine years past,
and still, you grace me.

The words that were written
didn't really make sense
but they were rhythmic and poetic
and we heard them and felt them
and knew they were true
somewhere, somehow ringing through—
ringing through layers of dust from our trudging,
ringing through to me and you.

Socked in, they say,
of low-lying fog
breezing past my windows.
Floating in a cloud, I say,
as I raise my sights
to clear skies above
and gaze down with pleasure
at the misty realm
breathing its soft breath across the land,
as I drift down
to the deep-throated music
of ship calls sounding their way,
as I rest serene in wispy softness.

If I'm not pretty,
if I don't know the games of allure,
what is it that makes you love me?

It's the whole of you, you say, body and soul,
that either attracts me or doesn't,
and if it does, then your toes arouse me,
the way you move seduces me,
your scent is the spice of life,
your glance causes me to swoon,
the length of your nose,
the imperfection of your complexion
All stir tenderness in me.
If I do not recognize you, body and soul,
beauty and knowing the art of allure cannot hold me,
your toes, your scent, your glance, the way you move
are mute to my senses, my heart,
the length of your nose, your complexion
become an unappealing distraction.

But, oh, my sweet,
do not fear,
I love the whole of you, body and soul.

"Lay low" is the advice
when threat hovers
like shimmering heat
on the horizon.
So when there are those
who show themselves,
who gather together,
wave banners, shout realities,
sound clarions for justice,
laying low disappears,
courage shimmers
boldly,
change dances
into a new day.

❧

Trailing through hanging vines, the scent of blossoms in the air.
Wending through forests, ancient giants, lacy ferns.
Crossing desert sands, sun blazing heat.
Weathering mountain passes, numbing cold of wind, rain, sleet.
Joy radiant with promise rendered leaden with despair.
Love's embrace rent to tatters in life's fierce storms.
Encircled in strong arms. Love persevering.
Slammed by death's heavy hand. Drifting alone.
All the while, there we are,
bundled together in good times and bad,
dancing in moonlight, singing lusty songs.
Not even death's knell prevents your riding on the breath of cool air,
wafting generously in the scent of blossoms in my hair.

Sweetly, secretly,
yellow footfalls
pad stealthily, boldly,
stalking through tall grasses,
rounding corners,
entering unfamiliar doorways,
to toss and tussle,
exuberate, betray,
move forward
pad softly
upright, known,
confident, sure-footed,
stumbling, searching
in the yellow dawn
and rosy twilight
surrendered fortuitous,
oh, journey to the sea.

⌒⌒

Words they used in talking about
Making Books were irresistible words.
They said that books themselves, and the urgency to write them,
are a Beautiful Absurdity. They said that the urgency to write is
Imagination That Wants To Materialize.
Making Books
Beautiful Absurdity
Imagination That Wants To Materialize
What wonderful words these—
what wonderful, wonderful words—
they reach in and pull up an essence
which resonates so wonderfully. So wonderfully
that to materialize them in a poem waxes urgent.

To see a three-year-old
in full, joyous concentration
place stones just so
around a broken pipe
is to see the sweet artist in us all.

꧁꧂

Rainbow promise
scattering its pot of gold
in the warmth of your eyes,
the pleasure of your hands,
a rascally rascal
who broke my heart,
gathered up its pieces,
melded them together
with a soft touch,
a steadfast hand,
love holding us strong
from our lusty youth
to your dying day.

Sing high
Sing free
Sing of your love
for me

Sing low
Sing deep
I'll sing my love
for thee

Sing wide
Sing sweet
We'll sing our love
high and low and deep

Curled for rest,
the window opened to the night,
cool air's caress
untangling knotted fright,
the brow unfurls,
corners of the mouth lift,
the soft breeze,
a breath into slumber sweet.

Let us dance in the meadow.
Let us stroll through the woods.
Let us climb to the mountaintop
and wander the valley.
Let us join hands in sweet camaraderie,
shout our pain and lack of understanding,
shout our joy and connectedness,
sing our songs of victory and pleasure.
Let us be a people together.

When I leave this world
maybe I'll leave as a burst of light,
a bright new star in the universe of life.
Or, rather, I may be a speck of dust
whirled by the wind to join earth's vast plains.
I may be a somber tolling deep-throated bell.
Perhaps I'll stalk away, a great silent cat,
or I'll bound from this world as a shy gazelle
leaping through tall grass.
I could be carried into quiet oblivion, disappear entirely,
or I might enter a world filled with new learning.
However I leave, when I leave this world as leave I surely will,
I'll leave it mournfully in a long last bid adieu to
its beauty, its agony, its wonder, its joy.